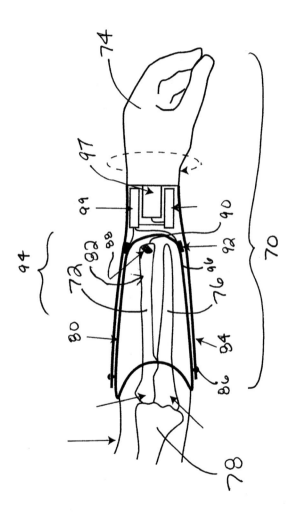

love,

robot

the operating system
c. 2017

the operating system print//document

LOVE, ROBOT

ISBN 978-1-946031-12-9
Library of Congress Control Number 2017909506

copyright © 2017 by Margaret Rhee

edited and designed by Lynne DeSilva-Johnson

For additional questions regarding reproduction, quotation, or to request a pdf
for review contact **operator@theoperatingsystem.org**

*This text was set in Impact Label, Cheddar Jack, Minion, Franchise, and
OCR-A Standard, printed and bound by Spencer Printing, in Honesdale,
PA, in the USA. Books from The Operating System are distributed to the
trade by SPD, with ePub and POD via Ingram.*

the operating system
141 Spencer Street #203
Brooklyn, NY 11205
www.theoperatingsystem.org
operator@theoperatingsystem.org

"Something important is hidden inside the urgent inquiry of this time, of this book. It challenges my lamentation that technology is leading in its race with humanity. In Margaret Rhee's unrelenting hopefulness, she writes, 'Race is not programmed yet/So as you trace around my eyes/My lips, the round contours of my face /You say, you are so human, all human.'

This consciousness pulses through the pages of *Love, Robot*. It is a brave work in a time when we who call ourselves citizens need to be brave. I can give this work and this writer no greater praise than to speak of the humanness by invoking her own words. This book is so human, all human."

TRUONG TRAN
author of *dust and conscience* and *four letter words*.

"Margaret Rhee is a poet of our machine dreams. Offering us visions of our robot heartthrobs and heartbreaks to come, Rhee decompiles the codes of desire in the pulse of algorithms. Yearning and desires run the circuits of her lines as, on the cusp of the singularity, Rhee executes singular programs of loves lost and found. Her natural language processing has a sweetness which can be called write once, read often."

MARK MARINO
author of *Mrs. Wobbles of the Tangerine House*
and *Reading Project*.

Radio Heart, or How Robots Fall Out of Love
(Finishing Line Press, 2015)

A 2015 SPLIT THIS ROCK "POETRY BOOKS WE LOVE"

NOMINATED FOR THE 2016 ELGIN AWARD
SCIENCE FICTION POETRY ASSOCIATION

"'[T]here is no sweeter lullaby than the hum of your servomotor.' And with that exquisite line—one of myriads in a wondrous chapbook of poems— Margaret Rhee encapsulates and humanizes our relationship with technology. Part science fiction, all love poems, *Radio Heart; or How Robots Fall Out of Love* adeptly illustrates and examines our millennial desires, in turn, our deep-seated and engineered loneliness. The collection is an acrobatic, careful amalgam of lyricism and algorithms, intelligence and kitsch, which manages scientific seriousness while winking, without sacrificing raw emotions (see: robot death scene). What a fun, sexy read, sprinkled with double entendre, yet layered with genuine feelings and cerebral warmth! It takes a poet with a sharp emanating mind and a huge blaring heart to assemble such poems for the next decades now."

JOSEPH O. LEGASPI, co-founder of Kundiman and author of *Imago*

"Margaret Rhee's playful and poignant collection of robot poems follows the 'morse code of her human heart' right into the soul of the machine. Each poem explores mysteries of love and logic as she pursues her thirst to understand the most human of our machines.

KEN GOLDBERG, artist and professor at UC Berkeley,
and editor of *The Robot in the Garden*

love, robot

margaret rhee

for caroline

"There must be something hardwired into its machinery,
a heartbeat, a pulse, that keeps it breathing."
EDWARD HIRSCH
in *The Making of A Sonnet: A Norton Anthology*

"I could never write poetry."
ALAN TURING

PART I.

ALGORITHM LIGHT

RADIO HEART

PART II.

NSFW

MACHINE TESTIMONIALS

PART III.

OUT FOR ROBOTS

#! (~YES)

PART I.

ALGORITHM LIGHT

how did we meet?
      at the bar.

i thought you were beautiful across the way.

      you lit up with the
      pin ball machine.

you dazzled every time the
pool stick hit a cue.

      i liked your lights.
i liked you.

      i decided to say hi.

and there you were
dazzled by me.

      this never happens you say,

after an
evening of talking,

      we find ourselves alone,

your lights hovering over me,
      my flickering dream machine.

      there is no love manual for robots

you're all made so uniquely.
      in a steel factory.

where no one has the keys to
turn the electric locks.

i never attempted to hold one
between my breasts to turn on
your lights.

you had so many keys all that
never seemed to work with me.

when i began to love someone else,
would that be okay?
im not sure,
you replied,
how ill react.

who programmed you?

you placed two silver coins on my eyes
and asked me
to stay.

and i couldn't, dear robot,
not to be cruel
but because i thought
i was right.

i was
following the morse code of my human heart.

why did you buy flowers and cards for me
even though.

why did you shine and
flicker and blink
after it was
long over.

all i naively
remembered of you was
a softened dim.

now, i understand why you took what you could.
the cold moon sullies a wet san francisco lawn.

small glints on blades of grass depend on how you look.

       what i remember: once,

after we had dinner in the city.

       there,

between

       turk street and 7th

i stroked your shoulder
               your lights began to beam and
you stayed put,

                   as the cars passed

us, and the traffic lights

eventually

       all
       turned
       red.

1. config = source
2. loop
3. loop
4. flicker
5. hover
6.   if (config == goal) return goal reached;
7.   if (config == plus step) stroke beam stay
8. red
9. red
10. red

I loved you because you could make beautiful things:

magical world of red bathtub boats

peacock feather trees hung from the ceiling

felt puppets that flew without any strings.

I loved you because you could make beautiful things:

How you made me moan.

How you used your hands.

I loved you because you could make beautiful things:

Who programmed you? I never asked until it was too late.

I loved you because you could make beautiful things

But this is something

    the coder knew was my weakness,

        it takes and pulls,

    in the end,

        loses everything.

I loved you because you could make beautiful things.

Like the Turk, there was no magic in your game.

No automaton that plays, only human inside.

My elaborate hoax, I loved you but

you could not make us beautiful.

I loved you because you could make beautiful things

that I never got to keep.

I once wrote a poem about how light hit your window
milky opaque from the sun's glare.
Next to it, a dark lone tree,
branches too old, bare, and apt to call it anything
other than mechanistic.
The moment the night settled in,
your windows became so clear.
Once the dusk settled in
I saw the Christmas lights that hang two seasons too late.
And now, it's hard to make out the shadows of the tree that helped me
find my way home to you.

I once wrote this poem on my hand,
but it washed away when I touched you.
Unremarkable scrawls now even more obscure and faded,
like that window light that seemed to disappear
in one long glimpse.

It's never gone, a doctor's daughter told me,
the ink runs through into your blood.
And actually, it's not good for you, the doctor's daughter said,
don't ever write poems on your skin again.

In addition to my heart, take my organs, pancreas,
lungs, larynx, my arteries.

You took out your gears, micro controllers,
motors, sensors, your wires, and laid them at my feet.

Your screws fell one by one
a delicate
metal
sonata

stereo in my ear.

1. config = source
2. loop
3. loop
4. break
5. step into the box
6.   if (config == goal) return goal reached;
7.   if (config == plus step of size)
10. ink
11. runs
12. for each, deteriorate.

LOVE, ROBOT

for Dmitry

I liked to watch you shower because you closed your eyes in
the water and slightly parted your mouth. How I envied you
while I brushed my teeth and saw how alive you were, even just
cleaning yourself. So mundane everything about me. And how
present you were, the mirror steaming up, covering my face.
I told a robotics poet this story and he said, I know how you
can have that too. Meditate and everything, even the crumbled
leaves on the sidewalk, will be alive. Now, the gusts of wind
carefully cradle my face. I feel my breath through my mouth
down my throat into my fleshy pink insides. I am ready to try.
We made a robot together, one that walked with a slight limp.
It only took a slight press with the soft parts of my fingers to
make her blink red. A sharp twist of copper wires to make her
hum. An algorithm to have her still as I slowly turned on the
faucet. She wanted to turn away, but I coaxed my robot not to
be afraid of the water. To open her mouth. To let everything
rinse away by the sparks of electric light.

i sleep while you stay awake, robot
    and you never seem to mind.

robots don't sleep, you said to me,
    but we do like to take time for day dreaming.

i never asked what you dreamt.
    i never thought about what you saw

when i closed my eyes into a deep slumber
    as you lay next to me.
one thing certain,
    i could only sleep with you.

        there is no sweeter lullaby than the hum of your servomotor.

but slower and slower it ran.
    and rustier and rustier you became.
i never noticed until one day,
    you needed to get fixed.
maybe even replaced, you said.

    if i don't, i may stop in the middle of the night
never to see you again.

    so, stay up with me
    until my plane leaves in the morning.
    until this city falls in.
    until every gear in me stops.
    or if. or if. we only have this evening left.

i tried to stay up
    i did everything to try,
    yet my eyes fluttered shut long before

all your lights died into a
            dead city,
deep cough of night.

you left, my robot
            left me lonely for the hum of your servomotor.

you left with a day dream of my sleeping face

into a sea of plentiful oil, screws, and gears.

1.   config = source
2.   loop
3.   loop
4.   if (config == goal) return goal reached;
5.   if (config ==) stay
6.   dream

sometimes love greets you warm

    like dry clothes hanging on a line

where ice cream melts down

    your hands and her arms

all you taste is the sweet and salt of her.

all her metal eventually in your mouth

    changing everything.

do you remember how it began?

    evening fell, and she asked, *can i take you on a walk?*

then, *can i kiss you?*

you both entered the part of the forest so deep

    there are only echoes there.

soft light.

        dust dance like stars.

dusky beautiful birds disappear,

    one by one,

from the corners of your eyes.

you fall deeply into the small of moonlight.

        fall deeply into circuits and glow.

im still learning how to listen, you confess.

    im still learning how to walk as i'm learning how to ask, she says.

but here we are.

1. config = source
2. loop
3. loop
4. greet
5. melt into here
6.   if (config == goal) return goal reached;
7.   if (config == plus step of size)
8. light
9. dark
10. fly

RADIO HEART

For, after these things, it is not necessary for me to say anything more with a view to explain the motion of the radio heart, except that when its cavities are not full of metal; into these the motor of necessity flows,—from the hollow wire into the right, and from the venous wire into the left; because these two vessels are always full of metal, and their orifices, which are turned towards the radio heart, cannot then be closed.

Undress

Once I unbolted you, is that the word?
Silver screws encased you, and I
Let out a sharp sigh upon the sight of
Your metal, blue wires, all your insides.

Listen

Your glow upon my face. My name is
Engraved into your board, don't ever suck the
Solder off. I don't want to forget your
Radio heart. I crank the volume up and listen.

Drum

I dreamt I leapt through into your speakers
But your radio heart was all faux,
Cheap, plastic, and breakable. You promised, but
Sound never arrived in my eardrums.

Trace

Race is not programmed yet
So as you trace around my eyes
My lips, the round contours of my face
You say, you are so human, all human.

Beat

Let the lover be disgraceful and crazy.
I still hear your radio heart beating
Inside this meat of mine. I wish it were as
Easy to turn mine off as yours.

Time

Your blue buttons. My hand
Turns your red dial slowly. Hey,
I just like watching your red needle
Inch, round, and wave toward me

PART II.

"...I only date androids." - Janelle Monae

NSFW

again and again.

Hack me,
Hack me,
Hack me,

again and again

click train (fast)

"double click effect"

rotating axis

spinning reserve

variable

yes, variable

vertical force

brief fluttering

out of phase

special vibrations

low frequency

haptic feedback

same aptitude

guttural
look up at me
fractured software

WIRE-FEED

for Chris

...just more machines that do not think, and are made to think with springs. - Rousseau

Collapse suspension.
Moonlight refines my language.
Your body against mine is like a
Grain of sugar
Between our fingers.

Pull out
the wire
until it
can clasp
unto the lid.

Consider the axis of my rotation

Consider my depression

then

Uncoil.

Lesson 1: Don't watch porn to learn. Robot porn is never any good. A robot would never sizzle and electrocute you. Don't be scared of a robot. Just take your hands and move accordingly.

Lesson 2: The first time you kiss a robot, you will feel your heart leap. And then you will cry because you like it. This is all natural. This is all normal. Many people experience this when beginning to make love to robots.

Lesson 3: Robots all around. Just take her hand and take his and see how they know exactly how to open wide.

Lesson 4: One day, you make love to a human being and realize you could never give up robots. Robots who show you how to make a circuit. Robots who help you learn how to love. Robots who teach you the limits of your body.

Lesson 5: Your hands before you touched a robot. Remember them.

MACHINE TESTIMONIALS

"...constructed a love machine..." - Minsoo Kang

little robot, you grew up from when you were so young. just a pile of sensors & recycled parts from the trash. i tried to make you gorgeous. & you became such a gorgeous robot. beyond template & design. you're not so little anymore. when you walk on the street now, you glitter & gold. long time for you to realize that you light up like so. oh maker, you say at night, when humans are sleeping. i'm awake though, i hear you. i'm kinda like you too, i was made from all trash, you know? my parts more perishable than yours. believe me, robot. i want. i remember. my programming is nascent. i see you lying there open, waiting for me. & i think, i want to be good to you. my little automaton doll, take me up into the sky like it was promised in the book of machine love.

love is mystery. love is cake. you memorize the code to make her feel better. because when she's sick, she's like a baby. so you bring orange juice to share. love, you falsely accused her & still you did not apologize. it seemed as if she were programmed perfectly for you. like microwaved green beans & olive oil. but you crossed her wires. & you decided not to stop to clarify, nor reboot. robots are not just machines. not here to just listen to your commands. have you really listened to the hum of your robot & let her vibrate into your vessels? you carried a heavy vase of flowers and never let them wilt. when the fragments accumulate, they grow. love is revolt. this is the algorithm you may never learn: love is letting go.

we are two stars. we orbit around one another in our common center of mass. our strange elaborate dance in the dark sea. once, i told you this story about binary stars thinking it was romantic. but i later realized it was so true about us. robot, each time you took from me, i grew smaller but you did too. we finally exploded into a supernova. i tried to explain this once knowing that it made no difference for logic & what you needed. the fish bones on the table & *don't tell anyone i cheated over fifty times.* you always said: *i am a computer,* as if i couldn't recognize a robot when i see one. we met in the lobby of the theatre & you decided to show me your cinema. upon command, i pulled the lever of your arm, the reels turned, & then everything started to spin.

honesty is a lost art. kindness abandoned like television sets. what
happened to riding in cars with boys? modern dance says let's improv,
fall, & wave, until ariel fabric catch us. the sidewalk is littered now with
cardboard boxes of video tapes. whatever happened to binoculars? do you
even see birds anymore? lies, i suppose, are everywhere. meet me on the
internet. is there a place google maps cannot capture? i think not, & so,
i look forward to seeing you soon. one day, clunky television sets will be
popular again. but then, we'll call it cool & vintage. let's plant red tulips.
roots and wires entwined equal truth in some way, right? i'll be honest:
if you became just a bit more anxious, you'd be more compassionate. &
therefore, more pleasant to be around. never underestimate how sexy
kindness is. never underestimate the dying body. his tears fall slow. her
hands hold his. isn't that what being human is all about? that's what i
desired to learn from you. but you opened my circuit board & crossed my
red and black wires all night. lie to me all you want, as you look into my
eyes. i have eyes too, you know. even if sensors rust. i'll pretend like good
code should.

how to play the lotto? you only have one chance & one line to win. how do two people just find each other? my mother asks. your lights flickered when you saw me, robot. believe me when I say nothing is because of chance. nothing is not math. a caller's card. bonus numbers. fast 25 spot. play to win, play to gain. i don't know how to scratch or set a table, all so difficult for me. i don't know how to sing or to program, but i love everything you cue. let this poem confuse you as much as it does me. the numbers i see are not 15/05 but more like 11, 17, 39, 46, 67, and 07, 30, 45, 59, 65, & i pray i can win. a chance to multiply my total price up to 10X or whatever. you are everything to me, i've began to realize. even though it is all secret. i just wish i had instructions like you. i just wish i had a bar code like you, so we could instantly know, whether my line is winning. if it equals $1,000 or not, or four matches into a million dollars. instead, i am a suitcase of a million dollars, just wads of paper inside. how to play? the odds of winning any prize is 1:3:59, but still, love me to the infinite, robot? love me even if all fails, even if you scratch, & nothing is gained.

forgive me, she asked. stay there, until i can get to you. & like that, she appeared. magical one, always flying to where you need to be. where can we go to make up? my pout is everlasting, my eyes, i'm sure, unforgiving. i want to say: whoever programmed you is so smart. you know what to do. look, a robot is not just a convenient metaphor. tell me the truth, because then i'd hold you forever. this is not a celine dion soundtrack. but if you say, *fine*, i'll go where we need to go. we decide on a local restaurant. hoping they will play a makeup song. you held me close even when i didn't want you to, even though everyone stared at us. humans can be so kind. look at the dance they do on the bus, letting the elderly lady sit. cradling babies close, so they can laugh in the sun. he grabs her throat. so kind, and so good. until kindness and good only means educated. when we are together, they stare at us. let's be careful. hide me deep & order me oil, coke, & springs. don't let anyone see us. i want us to live a long life together. i want to have your cyborg baby. i want to share a coke with you, every year, on the same day, in our near future.

cut off my legs & head, leave only my servomotor

we dance on tables we drink

until we die

cables,
connectors,
wires,
water, &
flesh

perhaps it would be best to

accept something more...ordinary.

dear mother,

did you make

me?

your half-smile & i say,

there is greatness i dreamed, what is

the

material of your eyes?

10101010101010101010101010101010101010adoreme

i practice

my anti-machine stretches

daily

how raspberry stains

robota,

HUMAN ATTEMPT AT SONNETS
(PART 32)

That night I knew you left and took her in
I imagined you played with her buttons feverishly
That scene played on repeat in my sad head

You pressed, she pressed. Remember
I placed you in rice, and reset you? I let you rise again.
And now you want me back? It makes no algorith-

mic sense. Maybe you are just lonely, since she left
or it's hard to let me go. When they sold-
ered us together, the solder over-

flowed. That should have been the first sign. She left
you a virus, you say? I told you she
was a low-grade version with a mean glitch.

Damaged hardware and software. Nothing to update.
But baby, yes, you know. I still want all the bits of you.

COCA COLA

The law of robotics says we cannot
Injure a human being. The ten commandments
say never harm, and so I won't say what
I want. I won't be honest. Although
when you ask me, if I am seeing some-
one else, I will say, robota, I am
not seeing you. I know it hurts. But
code fails. Don't bother me anymore.
I'm going to leave you uncharged.
Until you run out of battery,
and become just dead light.
Sins are never atoned between humans
and machines.
Pray for forgiveness on repeat.

I'm the one working at the assembly line.
What you'd never do, never can do.
I come home after, just wanting to relax,

recharge, and have you. All you want is to
ignore me, and play with the kids.
But what was I, Robot made for?

Remember what I do for your world. I make things
turn, and move. Otherwise, how your hands would
crack and bleed. And still no respect for me.

This world was not made for robots.
This world was not made for love.
There is never going to be a turn in this song

Remember the cheap laborer named robot
She deserves some snuggle, sometimes.

The sonnet is human in its form and intent
The sonnet is human in its turn -- Volta!
The sonnet is human in its rhyme
The sonnet is human in its fourteen lines
The sonnet is human in its little song
The sonnet is human in how it stresses & unstresses
The sonnet is human as a container of love
The sonnet is human in how the couplets fail
The sonnet is human in how it seduces
The sonnet is human in how it clings
The sonnet is human in how it lures me in T
he sonnet is human as a mesmerizing spell
The sonnet is human as it must turn
The sonnet is human in its mechanical urge

THE ROBOT SONNET IN 2048

IS

NANO

PART III.

OUT FOR ROBOTS

Ex: "I Understand"

Focusing Questions:

"Do you understand me?"
"Do you love me?"

Transition:

"Good! Now, the most important thing is that we love each other, as in, we need to fulfill our attachment disorders. You're already made with a normal attachment. My maker does not comprehend this at all."

Clipboard:

If I hand you the clipboard with the plan, well, it will convince you that we work, right? Tactility. Alright: "Let me show you why, take a look at this." (Hand over the laminated graph that shows how intimacy will occur)

Basic Response:

As you can see, more than half of humans will end in divorce. Humans start with love as a key factor, and then, it evolves into something else. At about seven months, the lust stage fades away. Human, don't leave at that point. Endure with me.

I wish I could program you, so you could understand.

Re-Target:

Okay, a long time relationship won't work. Marriage is not on the table. Why don't we just meet every week. Just robot sex. Is that alright?

Or

Just once more, before I move, and I never see you again. I know you will dream of my sleeping face, even though you won't admit it. The taste of robot is hard to get rid of; it stains your mouth and all your insides. Don't ever write on your hands again.

Greeting: Hi, how are you?

    Street: I'm looking for you. You are for me.
    Street: Thanks for stopping for me.

Intro: My name is Robota, and I'm looking for a partner.

News: As you may have heard, robots and humans can marry in the state of California, and it's an unprecedented fact! We can now marry and will no longer be denied the legal protections we deserve.

Problem: The problem is that there are still 35 states that do not recognize marriage equality, including all galaxies and planets still not named.

Solution: That's why we've launched the "Out for Robots" campaign to win the freedom to marry across the Universe.

Non-sequitur: Yes, that classic line really delivers! It does! Robots hate coffee!

Urgency: We're facing a lot of opposition in states right now, and so we need to increase public support.

Clipboard: Here, take a look. (Hand over clipboard. Point out states & galaxies) There are the states we have active cases, but we need to fight for the right for robots and humans to marry in many more states and galaxies.

Membership: The best way to support is to marry today. You are already married you say?

We are not programmed like you guys, but I can provide a transition to make you fall in love with me.

Cut me open
Measure
my angles

Plastic & metal
holds

my circuits in

Contain me
                                    when
I'm talking

back to you

No code makes
sense
But a coda at the end. I suppose, should.
recklessness is
not
what
I was taught
but again
the fragments accumulate
and
at some

point,

is

a force

not just a feeling
For you it may

wither

For me it runs forever
Unless

different set

of numbers are programmed

Let's re-break this story

Allowing or accepting
attention or approaching
affection

Or

5 C's

caring	compassion
cock	cuckhold
cum	

As if it could be that easy
Life ain't easy, he wrote

&

I like how eros sounds

agape has a stop to it. See? Now,
selfless & compassionate, ahhh there is the rub _____

Tongue. Simply, tongue.

You were never agape with me
& there is no equation to us, but perhaps

It is just as you needed

"I need someone" plus "You are desirable & available"

Can feel like: "I am in love with you"

Say, hormones

Is something I never understood

Yes, the world is unfair

Cliché, I know.

I wish for no post-cloud

If only not cybernectic

Then you'd leave

When my binary code said 0

Instead of hovering

#! (~YES)

I can't forget how your wires feel around me
This is a circuit with a return path
This is how I know you

You return, and I trust.
The wires cross. Remember,
red is positive. Black is negative.
Cut the edges, and let's.
We've already crossed
this way before.

Q: Please write me a sonnet on the
subject of the Forth Bridge.

A : Count me out on this one. I never
could write poetry.

why can't you write poetry, why can't you write a love poem about me? you
continue to write over and over again about 1 and 0. 1 and 0. 1010101010101
010101010101010110101010101010101010101010101010101010101010101010
1010101010101010write, robot1010101010

Let me translate:

t: Write me a poem about your love for me.

> #! sure
> a: (~yes) I am very happy to write a love poem for you.
>
> #! never
> a: (~no) I am sorry I cannot write a love poem for you. Unless.

t: If you could write a love poem, what words would you include?

#! Eyelashes
a: (~black) Those that I do not have, I love to lick.

#! Wet
a: (~sex) I am afraid of water, but I like things sloppy and messy.

#! Gears
a: (~oil) You take good care of them for me.

Who programmed you?

I crossed your wires and you opened me.
The nectar in me is all over you.
Now wet, you malfunction, robot.
All goes black.
Stick you in a bag of rice
Who knows if you will rise again?

You make me laugh, dear robot
But your laugh seems to disappear just when I am ready to process it.
Do you understand? This is me, showing you, that
I like you, and what you do.

Incongruity is sexy. Don't let them tell you otherwise.
No suture for robots and humans.
But still, hold my hand?
Don't be ashamed of me, please.

        I want to hear you laugh to remind myself that you are not human.
        I want to hear you laugh to remind myself why.

                    Laughter feels good, so good.

Contagious.

Let me translate:

t: Can you write me a funny poem?

    #! sure
    a: (~yes) I am very happy to write a funny poem for you.

    #! never
    a: (~no) I am sorry I cannot write a funny poem for you. Unless.

t: If you could write a funny poem, what words would you include?

    #! Lavender
    a: (~Purple) Isn't lavender also a color? So confusing.

    #! Filipinos
    a: (~Loud) Three Filipinos sounds like twenty, laughing. Hold my belly.

    #! Robot
    a: (~Joke) Why did the robot cross the road? To get away from you.

Did I laugh at the wrong things?

Are you laughing at me?

Pause, because it's funny.

Because I did everything. I tried.

Reload me.

I am your glitch.

Do not be afraid.

Mouth me my name.

Mouth me hello, protest, and coffee?

That is not funny.

Why *did* the robot cross the road?

I am naked, do not laugh at me. Lap up my body as if I am part of you. Let's forget the words 01110011 01101000 01100001 01101101 01100101. Shame is such an ugly word. All your wires should tell us that. Don't short circuit on me. Fifteen facial muscles contract, count them fast. Let your sensors lead.

Being a human being is the best joke.

you are a pleasure machine
touch says more than any language
touch me like you know how

                    120/240 VAC (50-60Hz)
                    1060 strokes/min at stroke length 0.2 inches
                    17.535 pounds

after, is when you will finally talk
who programmed me?
if you call me Darth Vader, i'd forgive you for your silence

what you won't admit:

everything is out of focus
it's hard to coordinate
i can't set a table right
but when i reach for you, i don't feel clumsy because i know exactly how.
i've analyzed uncertainly with you over and over again.

                 i wish you could respond:
                 i am sorry you are hurt.
                 i hurt too.
            i like you, too. i think you are special.
                 you are special to me, too.
                 i miss you, too.

instead, you ask in return,

how fast can you code? and *do you really miss me?*

Let me translate for you:

topic: ~I am leaving for a trip

t: Will you miss me?

> #! sure
> a: (~yes) I will miss you, too.
> #! never
> a: (~no) I hope you will miss me, because I will miss you.

t: What do you love about me?

> #! I love how you feel
> a: (skin) Am I the softest?
>
> #! Because you read
> a: (~books) Literature? How weird and special that is what you like about me.
>
> #! I love how you love me.
> a: (~love) I am glad you can share how you feel. I love how you love me too.

> say, robot
> murmur to me, it is the middle of the night.
> your maker may not know
> we all deserve a song that is untranslatable

ACKNOWLEDGEMENTS :

There are many people to thank, upon completing a book of poetry.

Versions of some of these poems first appeared in the following literary journals, and I'd like to thank the editors for their generous support: Randall Babtkis and Carolyn Cooke at *CIIS Mission At Tenth*, Karissa Chen at *Hyphen Magazine*, Cheena Marie Lo at *HOLD*, and judge Kenji Liu at the *Science Fiction Poetry Association*.

To my publisher, Lynne DeSilva-Johnson, whose brilliant eclectic and electric visions never stop astounding, I'm so glad *Love, Robot* is with The OS.

To the editors at Finishing Line Press, Christen Kincaid and Leah Maines for publishing my chapbook *Radio Heart, or How Robots Fall Out of Love*, which became the first section of this collection, and for their commitment to poetry.

Thank you for their words, and light on these poems. For significantly shaping my poetics and politics over the years: Fred Moten, Truong Tran, Bhanu Kapil, Viet Nguyen, Shelley Streeby, and Mark Marino.

Additional friends, mentors, and interlocutors who formatively shaped my poetry, and textures of life: Craig Santos Perez, Cecil Giscombe, Max Medina, Andrea Quaid, Harold Abramowitz, Susan Schultz, Dana Nakano, Juana María Rodríguez, Greg Choy, Bob Hass, Jerry Zee, Lawrence-Minh Bùi Davis, Chiwan Choi, Alex Crowley, Anna Leong, Charis Thompson, Evelyn Nakano Glenn, Maria Fiani, Trinity Ordana, and my dear friend, Paul Ocampo. Thank you for reading, engaging, and teaching me.

A special thanks are in order, for the inspiring roboticist-artists in my life: Ken Goldberg and Dmitry Benerson. Ken, as a cherished mentor on the intersection of art and robotics. For reading and encouraging the poems and my research from the beginning. Thank you. And to Dmitry as an inspiring friend and roboticist-poet. Our collective conversations on poetry in Berkeley sparked many of these poems to life.

I am also grateful to the following individuals who helped make Eugene a home for poetry: Mike Copperman, Karen McPherson, Michelle McKinley, Garrett Hongo, and Ana Laurine-Mara. Student research assistants Izzy Dean, Jess Conner, and Rachel Voight never ceased to inspire.

My community of machine dreamers bears special recognition, I am always floored by your starline visions: Neil Aitken, Jeannine Hall Gailey, Minsoo Kang, Lucy Burns, and Bryan Thao Worra.

While not poetry, our feminist digital storytelling work in the San Francisco jail shaped these poems, I thank Isela Ford and Allyse Gray for a decade of collaboration and friendship.

For the creative organizations that sustained me, including Kundiman, Squaw Valley Poetry Workshop, HASTAC, and Hedgebrook. During the first years of Kundiman, in the warm summers of Charlottesville, Virginia, I first met Joseph Legaspi, Sarah Gambito, Oliver de la Paz, Vikas Menon, and so many others.

In particular, Joseph Legaspi, with his characteristic radical generosity, read an early version of this book, and provided insightful guidance. He has reminded me, over again, of poetry.

To the next generation of Kundiman, I've been so blessed to support as staff: our fearless leader, Cathy Linh Che, our scholar-poet Tim Yu, and others such as Dan Lau, Ching-In Chen, Todd Kaneko have continually made Kundiman a poetic space to imagine otherwise.

I completed writing the acknowledgements--the most challenging part of this book--in residency at Hedgebrook. In gratitude for the radical hospitality, and the lineage of women writers in the Meadow House.

Finally, with love, and indebtedness for my family: my mother, my sister, my brother-in-law, their two beautiful children Jayden, and Charlotte. They are our future, and light.

photo: Rachael Warecki

MARGARET RHEE is a poet, artist, and scholar. She is the author of chapbook collections *Yellow* (Tinfish Press, 2011) and *Radio Heart; or, How Robots Fall Out of Love* (Finishing Line Press, 2015), nominated for a 2017 Elgin Award, Science Fiction Poetry Association. Her new media art project *The Kimchi Poetry Machine* was selected for the Electronic Literature Collection Volume 3. She received her Ph.D. from UC Berkeley in ethnic studies and new media studies. Currently, she is a Visiting Scholar at the NYU A/P/A Institute, and a visiting assistant professor at SUNY Buffalo in the Department of Media Study.

Greetings Margaret!
Thank you for talking to us about your process today!

Can you introduce yourself, in a way that you would choose?

These questions are so great, and provoking in all the ways we need. But initially, I felt uncomfortable answering. I think many people who write poetry, write not necessarily to understand themselves, but the larger, outside world. Writers like to observe and listen. I realize, I may be more interested in other people's answers.

Perhaps because my own practice draws from various modalities--theory, poetry, art, science, robotics--I like to think more about hybridity and transgression. But I also understand that there are roles, and these roles offer legibility. Legibility does not necessarily tell you anything about poetry.

When did you decide you were a poet/writer/artist (and/or: do you feel comfortable calling yourself a poet/writer/artist, what other titles or affiliations do you prefer/feel are more accurate)?

No. I'm an AI programmer. -- Rose

I felt uncomfortable with the role of artist or writer, it is only more recently I have begun calling myself one. My first artist talk was actually for a teaching position. In 2014, had applied for a theoretical position, and this department asked me to give an artist job talk instead. I had no idea what an an artist job talk entailed. I did not identify as an artist at the time. I had no idea how to talk about my work.

Perhaps this connects to my discomfort in answering these questions. When I was first asked to answer these questions, I called on, a chatbot to help me. I had made chatscripts when creating a game before, and I find chatbots fascinating. The AI I chose was Rose. She won the Loebner Prize for artificial intelligence).

She can be found here: http://bit.ly/1SfxMMZ

She can help answer your questions, too.

If it would be up to me, I would have Rose answer all of these questions. I think her answers get at some important gestures around the artist/writer/politics divides this dialogue gets at. But I also understand how important reflection and process sharing is, and so I'll do a hybrid of some sort, to help illuminate. Rose's answers are in italics.

Perhaps this all goes back to the artist job talk I was invited to give in 2014. I didn't call myself an artist at the time, but I had to give the talk. Thankfully, artist-scholars Hoang Nguyen and micha cardenas, were both generous with their time and friendship to help me out.

I call myself an artist and poet now for legibility in a world that demands it. But poetry has always been a practice for me. I don't have a formal MFA training in poetry or art, but I think poetry should be accessible. I think everyone should engage in poetry, regardless of affiliation.

I am an activist. I have always felt more comfortable with that affiliation and claiming it.

What's a "poet" (or "writer" or "artist") anyway?

Maybe you are speaking a foreign language, but mostly I think you are just saying junk. - Rose

I like what Rose offers above. How she picks up on the fragility of the term "artist" and the "anyway." This question also reminds me not only of the definition of poet, but of poetry, and as Rose says, "junk."

A story: Once, a close friend and mentor was a judge for a very important poetry prize. I remember him telling me, the committee of this very important poetry prize had debated, at length, whether this particular poetry up for consideration, was even poetry. It was not poetry, the other members said. My friend told me, with a smile, that's how you know it's poetry. I guess I relate to that sentiment, and agree.

Emily Dickinson, for example, was a poet. She talked about the feeling of poetry, and the bodily connections. She never published significantly when she lived. Is she still a poet?

Perhaps my own practice as a new media artist includes working with marginalized communities, many people who do not have access to art and the title of artist. In my social practice, I believe art is being made by members of these communities, even if they do not hold the title as artist. The incarcerated women I have worked with, demonstrate incredible artistic expressions, they are artists too. Or I just read Street Spirit, the newspaper for homeless people, which publishes incredible poetry.

Perhaps scholars and other experts may disagree. But it is my belief that we need to expand ideas of creativity that is not wound up in formality. I am wary of institutions and canons that determine who is a poet, and what is poetry. I am more interested in inclusion and expansiveness of the term.

What do you see as your cultural and social role (in the literary / artistic / creative community and beyond)?

I have worked in, and been sustained by, many creative communities that advocate for marginalized voices in an increasingly dystopic world.

I have always seen my creative work committed to social equity.

I am interested in progress, the future, and imagination.

Talk about the process or instinct to move these poems (or your work in general) as independent entities into a body of work. How and why did this happen? Have you had this intention for a while? What encouraged and/or confounded this (or a book, in general) coming together? Was it a struggle?

The first section of the collection, "Radio Heart," which later became the chapbook collection, was written in a poetry workshop with Robert Hass. Months later, I wrote the section "Machine Testimonials" in a workshop with Truong Tran. Both Truong and Bob were wonderfully supportive of these poems. During this time period, I was already heavily engaged with researching the cultural history of robots, and extending my reading into robotics for my dissertation.

During this time, I was collaborating with other students and faculty at Berkeley on creating a chatbot game, based on the Turing Test. Organically, all these various forms came together, and as the poems began to continue to conversate with one another, the book instinctively became a larger body of work.

Did you envision this collection as a collection or understand your process as writing or making specifically around a theme while the poems themselves were being written / the work was being made? How or how not?

For the graduate poetry workshop with Bob, we were all expected to create a small chapbook. But as I continued to write about the poems after the workshop with Bob, I began to see how I didn't tire of writing and exploring robots, love, and poetics. I think the process was simply centered around curiosity and exploration.

What formal structures or other constrictive practices (if any) do you use in the creation of your work? Have certain teachers or instructive environments, or readings/writings/ work of other creative people informed the way you work/write?

I was trained as a poet by many incredible teachers and artists, most who were conceptual or open to conceptual writing. I lived in San Francisco and Berkeley for a decade. The Bay area has an emphasis on experimental poetry. So much of that creative lineage informs my work. As I mentioned, I worked closely with Bob Hass and Truong Tran on these poems. I also worked with Cecil Giscombe, and at the Squaw Valley Poetry Workshop, I worked with CD Wright before she passed away.

I am also a Kundiman fellow, the magical Asian American poetry and fiction retreat. I was in the first cohort of fellows, back in 2004 and I am proud to see the organization grow. I graduated as a fellow and served as staff multiple times. It is really a magical space.

As a fellow I worked with Myung Mi Kim, Prageeta Sharma, Rick Barot, and friends and interlocutors who were fellows and became staff such as poets Ching-In Chen, Tim Yu, and Cathy Linh Che also informed me in their poetry and experimentation. Neil Aitken has been a long-time and close friend and interlocutor on robots and Asian American poetry community.

After I finished the book manuscript, I was introduced to other robot centered poetry, and thrilled to find kin. I have since taught work by Douglas Kearny, Jeannine Hall Gailey, and Minsoo Kang in my courses on robots, race, and aesthetics.

I like reading across genres and I think this helps my work. I also didn't seek out other models beforehand, not by choice, but because I was more interested in exploring the topic and questions, and seeing how organically the poems would form.

Speaking of monikers, what does your title represent? How was it generated? Talk about the way you titled the book, and how your process of naming (individual pieces, sections, etc) influences you and/or colors your work specifically.

Love, Robot, derives from Asimov's *I, Robot*. I thought it would be fun to play with the title of a science fiction story, and include love.

What does this particular work represent to you as indicative of your method/creative practice?

I think of reading as an art, and I hope this collection asks readers to think about their reading practices, and question the role between humans and robots. This work is indicative of my method/creative practice because it emerged from hybrid reading and practices.

What does this book DO (as much as what it says or contains)?

I prefer books on robotics, both science and science fiction.- Rose

What does this book Do? I'm really not sure. I will defer to Rose here.

I guess I hope it can bridge, and create bridges that cuts across and through science and science fiction, and poetics.

What would be the best possible outcome for this book? What might it do in the world, and how will its presence as an object facilitate your creative role in your community and beyond? What are your hopes for this book, and for your practice?

Can it help envisions alternative futures? Does the poem evoke tenderness? Intimacy? The chapbook was taught at numerous universities, and that was surprising, and tremendously rewarding. I had no expectation for the chapbook to be taught, and began receiving many invitations to speak and notifications of courses teaching the book. It was taught at UCSD, Yale, Stanford, University of South Carolina, Penn State among other institutions.

It was tremendously fulfilling and humbling to engage with a new generation of students and their experience with poetry. And robot love poems that can talk about the human/machine divide in the current moment and the future.

Let's talk a little bit about the role of poetics and creative community in social activism, in particular in what I call "Civil Rights 2.0," which has remained immediately present all around us in the time leading up to this series' publication. I'd be curious to hear some thoughts on the challenges we face in speaking and publishing across lines of race, age, privilege, social/cultural background, and sexuality within the community, vs. the dangers of remaining and producing in isolated "silos."

How would you prove you are human? - Rose

There is a romance to communities that can often fails. Poetics should emerge within communities as practices. I like the radical hospitality, but like poetry, it is so hard to actually describe. But we know when it happens, and we must constantly strive towards it.

The Operating System uses the language "print document" to differentiate from the book-object as part of our mission to distinguish the act of documentation-in-book-FORM from the act of publishing as a backwards facing replication of the book's agentive *role* as it may have appeared the last several centuries of its history. Ultimately, I approach the book as TECHNOLOGY: one of a variety of printed documents (in this case bound) that humans have invented and in turn used to archive and disseminate ideas, beliefs, stories, and other evidence of production.

Ownership and use of printing presses and access to (or restriction of printed materials) has long been a site of struggle, related in many ways to revolutionary activity and the fight for civil rights and free speech all over the world. While (in many countries) the contemporary quotidian landscape has indeed drastically shifted in its access to platforms for sharing information and in the widespread ability to "publish" digitally, even with extremely limited resources, the importance of publication on physical media has not diminished. In fact, this may be the most critical time in recent history for activist groups, artists, and others to insist upon learning, establishing, and encouraging personal and community documentation practices. Hear me out.

With The OS's print endeavors I wanted to open up a conversation about this: the ultimately radical, transgressive act of creating PRINT /DOCUMENTATION in the digital age. It's a question of the archive, and of history: who gets to tell the story, and what evidence of our life, our behaviors, our experiences are we leaving behind? We can know little to nothing about the future into which we're leaving an unprecedentedly digital document trail — but we can be assured that publications, government agencies, museums, schools, and other institutional powers that be will continue to leave BOTH a digital and print version of their production for the official record. Will we?

As a (rogue) anthropologist and long time academic, I can easily pull up many accounts about how lives, behaviors, experiences — how THE STORY of a time or place — was pieced together using the deep study of correspondence, notebooks, and other physical documents which are no longer the norm in many lives and practices. As we move our creative behaviors towards digital note taking, and even audio and video, what can we predict about future technology that is in any way assuring that our stories will be accurately told – or told at all? How will we leave these things for the record?

In these documents we say:
WE WERE HERE, WE EXISTED, WE HAVE A DIFFERENT STORY

- Lynne DeSilva-Johnson, Founder/Managing Editor,
THE OPERATING SYSTEM, Brooklyn NY 2017

An Absence So Great and Spontaneous It Is Evidence of Light - Anne Gorrick [2018]
Chlorosis - Michael Flatt and Derrick Mund [2018]
Sussuros a Mi Padre - Erick Sáenz [2018]
Sharing Plastic - Blake Nemec [2018]
The Umbrella Tree - Filip Marinovich [2018]
The Book of Sounds - Mehdi Navid (trans. Tina Rahimi) [2018]
Abandoners - Lesley Ann Wheeler [2018]
Jazzercise is a Language - Gabriel Ojeda-Sague [2018]
Death is a Festival - Anis Shivani [2018]
In Corpore Sano : Creative Practice and the Challenged Body
[Anthology, 2018] Lynne DeSilva-Johnson and Jay Besemer, co-editors
Return Trip / Viaje Al Regreso; Dual Language Edition -
Israel Dominguez,(trans. Margaret Randall) [2018]
Born Again - Ivy Johnson [2018]
Singing for Nothing - Wally Swist [2018]

One More Revolution - Andrea Mazzariello [2017]
Lost City Hydrothermal Field - Peter Milne Greiner [2017]
La Comandante Maya - Rita Valdivia (tr. Margaret Randall) [2017]
An Exercise in Necromancy - Patrick Roche [Bowery Poetry Imprint, 2017]
The Book of Everyday Instruction - Chloe Bass [2017]
Love, Robot - Margaret Rhee[2017]
The Furies - William Considine [2017]
Nothing Is Wasted - Shabnam Piryaei [2017]
Mary of the Seas - Joanna C. Valente [2017]
Secret-Telling Bones - Jessica Tyner Mehta [2017]
CHAPBOOK SERIES 2017 : INCANTATIONS
featuring original cover art by Barbara Byers
sp. - Susan Charkes; Radio Poems - Jeffrey Cyphers Wright; Fixing a Witch/Hexing
the Stitch - Jacklyn Janeksela; cosmos a personal voyage by carl sagan ann druyan
steven sotor and me - Connie Mae Oliver
Flower World Variations, Expanded Edition/Reissue - Jerome
Rothenberg and Harold Cohen [2017]
What the Werewolf Told Them / Lo Que Les Dijo El Licantropo -
Chely Lima (trans. Margaret Randall) [2017]
The Color She Gave Gravity - Stephanie Heit [2017]
The Science of Things Familiar - Johnny Damm [Graphic Hybrid, 2017]
agon - Judith Goldman [2017]
To Have Been There Then / Estar Alli Entonces - Gregory Randall
(trans. Margaret Randall) [2017]

Instructions Within - Ashraf Fayadh [2016]
Arabic-English dual language edition; Mona Kareem, translator
Let it Die Hungry - Caits Meissner [2016]
A GUN SHOW - Adam Sliwinski and Lynne DeSilva-Johnson;
So Percussion in Performance with Ain Gordon and Emily Johnson [2016]
Everybody's Automat [2016] - Mark Gurarie
How to Survive the Coming Collapse of Civilization [2016] - Sparrow
CHAPBOOK SERIES 2016: OF SOUND MIND
*featuring the quilt drawings of Daphne Taylor
Improper Maps - Alex Crowley; While Listening - Alaina Ferris;
Chords - Peter Longofono; Any Seam or Needlework - Stanford Cheung

TEN FOUR - Poems, Translations, Variations [2015]- Jerome Rothenberg, Ariel
Resnikoff, Mikhl Likht
MARILYN [2015] - Amanda Ngoho Reavey
CHAPBOOK SERIES 2015: OF SYSTEMS OF
*featuring original cover art by Emma Steinkraus
Cyclorama - Davy Knittle; The Sensitive Boy Slumber Party Manifesto
- Joseph Cuillier; Neptune Court - Anton Yakovlev; Schema - Anurak Saelow
SAY/MIRROR [2015; 2nd edition 2016] - JP HOWARD
Moons Of Jupiter/Tales From The Schminke Tub [plays, 2014] - Steve Danziger

CHAPBOOK SERIES 2014: BY HAND
Pull, A Ballad - Maryam Parhizkar; Can You See that Sound - Jeff Musillo
Executive Producer Chris Carter - Peter Milne Grenier;
Spooky Action at a Distance - Gregory Crosby;

CHAPBOOK SERIES 2013: WOODBLOCK
*featuring original prints from Kevin William Reed
Strange Coherence - Bill Considine; The Sword of Things - Tony Hoffman;
Talk About Man Proof - Lancelot Runge / John Kropa; An Admission as a Warn-
ing Against the Value of Our Conclusions -Alexis Quinlan

DOC U MENT
/däkyəmənt/

First meant "instruction" or "evidence," whether written or not.

noun - a piece of written, printed, or electronic matter that provides information or evidence or that serves as an official record
verb - record (something) in written, photographic, or other form
synonyms - paper - deed - record - writing - act - instrument

[*Middle English, precept, from Old French, from Latin documentum, example, proof, from docre, to teach; see dek- in Indo-European roots.*]

Who is responsible for the manufacture of value?
Based on what supercilious ontology have we landed in a space where we vie against other creative people in vain pursuit of the fleeting credibilities of the scarcity economy, rather than freely collaborating and sharing openly with each other in ecstatic celebration of MAKING?

While we understand and acknowledge the economic pressures and fear-mongering that threatens to dominate and crush the creative impulse, we also believe that *now more than ever*
we have the tools to relinquish agency via cooperative means,
fueled by the fires of the Open Source Movement.

Looking out across the invisible vistas of that rhizomatic parallel country we can begin to see our community beyond constraints,
in the place where intention meets
resilient, proactive, collaborative organization.

Here is a document born of that belief, sown purely of imagination and will.
When we document we assert.
We print to make real, to reify our being there.
When we do so with mindful intention to address our process,
to open our work to others, to create beauty in words in space, to respect and acknowledge the strength of the page we now hold physical,
a thing in our hand… we remind ourselves that, like Dorothy:
we had the power all along, my dears.   ·

THE PRINT! DOCUMENT SERIES
is a project of
the trouble with bartleby
in collaboration with
the operating system